C000099060

THE ILLUSTRATED POETS

Christina Rossetti

EDITED BY
Daniel Burnstone

This edition first published by Parragon Books Ltd in
1995

Produced by
Magpie Books Ltd, 7 Kensington Church Court
London W8 4SP

Cover picture: *Head of a Nymph* by Sophie Anderson,
Roy Miles Gallery/Bridgeman Art Library. Illustrations
courtesy of: Christies Images; Mary Evans Picture Library.

ISBN 0 75250 046 5

A copy of the British Library Cataloguing in Publication
Data is available from the British Library.

Typeset by Hewer Text Composition Services, Edinburgh
Printed in Singapore by Printlink International Co.

Contents

Echo

Come to me in the silence of the night;
  Come in the speaking silence of a dream;
Come with soft rounded cheeks and eyes as
      bright
  As sunlight on a stream;
    Come back in tears,
O memory, hope, love of finished years.

O dream how sweet, too sweet, too bitter
     sweet,
  Whose wakening should have been in
     Paradise,
Where souls brimfull of love abide and meet;

Where thirsting longing eyes
   Watch the slow door
That opening, letting in, lets out no more.

Yet come to me in dreams, that I may live
   My very life again though cold in death:
Come back to me in dreams, that I may give
   Pulse for pulse, breath for breath:
     Speak low, lean low,
As long ago, my love, how long ago.

18 *December* 1854.

Remember

Remember me when I am gone away,
  Gone far away into the silent land:
  When you can no more hold me by
      the hand,
Nor I half turn to go yet turning stay.
Remember me when no more day by
      day
  You tell me of our future that you
      plann'd:
  Only remember me; you understand

It will be late to counsel then or pray.
Yet if you should forget me for a while
    And afterwards remember, do not grieve:
    For if the darkness and corruption leave
    A vestige of the thoughts that once I had,
Better by far you should forget and smile
    That that you should remember and be
        sad.

Song

When I am dead, my dearest,
   Sing no sad songs for me;
Plant thou no roses at my head,
   Nor shady cypress tree:
Be the green grass above me
   With showers and dewdrops wet
And if thou wilt, remember,
   And if thou wilt, forget.

I shall not see the shadows,
   I shall not feel the rain:
I shall not hear the nightingale
   Sing on as if in pain:

And dreaming through the twilight
   That doth not rise nor set,
Haply I may remember,
   And haply may forget.

One Sea-Side Grave

Unmindful of the roses,
    Unmindful of the thorn,
A reaper tired reposes
    Among his gathered corn:
    So might I, till the morn!

Cold as the cold Decembers,
    Past as the days that set,
While only one remembers
    And all the rest forget, –
    But one remembers yet.

Memory

I

I nursed it in my bosom while it lived,
   I hid it in my heart when it was dead.
In joy I sat alone; even so I grieved
   Alone, and nothing said.

I shut the door to face the naked truth,
   I stood alone – I faced the truth alone,
Stripped bare of self-regard or forms or ruth
   Till first and last were shown.

I took the perfect balances and weighed;
   No shaking of my hand disturbed the
      poise;
Weighed, found it wanting: not a word I
     said,
   But silent made my choice.

None know the choice I made; I make it
    still.
  None know the choice I made and broke
    my heart,
Breaking mine idol: I have braced my will
    Once, chosen for once my part.

I broke it at a blow, I laid it cold,
  Crushed in my deep heart where it used to
    live.
My heart dies inch by inch; the time grows
    old,
  Grows old in which I grieve.

II

I have a room whereinto no one enters
  Save I myself alone:
  There sits a blessed memory on a throne,
There my life centres;

While winter comes and goes – oh
      tedious comer! –
  And while its nip-wind blows;
  While bloom the bloodless lily and
      warm rose
Of lavish summer.

If any should force entrance he might see
      there
  One buried yet not dead,
  Before whose face I no more bow my
      head
Or bend my knee there;

But often in my worn life's autumn
      weather
  I watch there with clear eyes,
  And think how it will be in Paradise
When we're together.

Goblin Market

Morning and evening
Maids heard the goblins cry:
'Come buy our orchard fruits,
Come buy, come buy:
Apples and quinces,
Lemons and oranges,
Plump unpecked cherries,
Melons and raspberries,
Bloom-down-cheeked peaches,
Swart-headed mulberries,
Wild free-born cranberries,
Crab-apples, dewberries,
Pine-apples, blackberries,
Apricots, strawberries; –
All ripe together

In summer weather, –
Morns that pass by,
Fair eves that fly;
Come buy, come buy:
Our grapes fresh from the vine,
Pomegranates full and fine,
Dates and sharp bullaces,
Rare pears and greengages,
Damsons and bilberries,
Taste them and try:
Currants and gooseberries,
Bright-fire-like barberries,
Figs to fill your mouth,
Citrons from the South,
Sweet to tongue and sound to eye;
Come buy, come buy.'

★ ★ ★

Backwards up the mossy glen
Turned and trooped the goblin men,
With their shrill repeated cry,
'Come buy, come buy.'
When they reached where Laura was
They stood stock still upon the moss,
Leering at each other,
Brother with queer brother;
Signalling each other,
Brother with sly brother.
One set his basket down,
One reared his plate;
One began to weave a crown
Of tendrils, leaves, and rough nuts brown
(Men sell not such in any town);
One heaved the golden weight
Of dish and fruit to offer her:

'Come buy, come buy,' was still their cry.
Laura stared but did not stir,
Longed but had no money.
The whisk-tailed merchant bade her taste
In tones as smooth as honey,
The cat-faced purr'd,
The rat-paced spoke a word
Of welcome, and the snail-paced even
        was heard;
One parrot-voiced and jolly
Cried 'Pretty Goblin' still for 'Pretty
        Polly';
One whistled like a bird.

But sweet-tooth Laura spoke in haste:
'Good Folk, I have no coin;
To take were to purloin:

Come to me in the silence of the night;
Come in the speaking silence of a dream

I have no copper in my purse,
I have no silver either,
And all my gold is on the furze
That shakes in windy weather
Above the rusty heather.'
'You have much gold upon your head,'
They answered all together:
'Buy from us with a golden curl.'
She clipped a precious golden lock,
She dropped a tear more rare than pearl,
Then sucked their fruit globes fair or red.
Sweeter than honey from the rock,
Stronger than man-rejoicing wine,
Clearer than water flowed that juice;
She never tasted such before,
How should it cloy with length of use?

She sucked and sucked and sucked the
        more
Fruits which that unknown orchard bore;

She sucked until her lips were sore;
Then flung the emptied rinds away
But gathered up one kernel stone,
And knew not was it night or day
As she turned home alone.

Lizzie met her at the gate
Full of wise upbraidings:
'Dear, you should not stay so late,
Twilight is not good for maidens;
Should not loiter in the glen
In the haunts of goblin men.
Do you not remember Jeanie,
How she met them in the moonlight,
Took their gifts both choice and many,

Ate their fruits and wore their flowers
Plucked from bowers
Where summer ripens at all hours?
But ever in the noonlight
She pined and pined away;
Sought them by night and day,
Found them no more, but dwindled and
        grew grey;
Then fell with the first snow,
While to this day no grass will grow
Where she lies low:
I planted daisies there a year ago
That never blow.
You should not loiter so.'
'Nay, hush,' said Laura:
'Nay, hush, my sister:
I ate and ate my fill,
Yet my mouth waters still:

To-morrow night I will
Buy more;' and kissed her.
'Have done with sorrow;
I'll bring you plums to-morrow
Fresh on their mother twigs,
Cherries worth getting;
You cannot think what figs
My teeth have met in,
What melons icy-cold

Piled on a dish of gold
Too huge for me to hold,
What peaches with a velvet nap,
Pellucid grapes without one seed:
Odorous indeed must be the mead
Whereon they grow, and pure the
        wave they drink
With lilies at the brink,
And sugar-sweet their sap.'

The Last of England, Ford Maddox Brown

Golden head by golden head,
Like two pigeons in one nest
Folded in each other's wings,
They lay down in their curtained bed:
Like two blossoms on one stem,
Like two flakes of new-fall'n snow,
Like two wands of ivory
Tipped with gold for awful kings.
Moon and stars gazed in at them,
Wind sang to them lullaby,
Lumbering owls forebore to fly,
Not a bat flapped to and fro
Round their nest:
Cheek to cheek and breast to breast
Locked together in one nest.

Early in the morning
When the first cock crowed his warning,
Neat like bees, as sweet and busy,
Laura rose with Lizzie:
Fetched in honey, milked the cows
Aired and set to rights the house,
Kneaded cakes of whitest wheat,
Cakes for dainty mouths to eat,
Next churned butter, whipped up cream,
Fed their poultry, sat and sewed;
Talked as modest maidens should:
Lizzie with an open heart,
Laura in an absent dream,
One content, one sick in part;
One warbling for the mere bright day's
            delight,
One longing for the night.

Remember me when I am gone away,
Gone far away into the silent land

The World

By day she woose me, soft, exceeding fair:
    But all night as the moon so changeth she;
    Loathsome and foul with hideous leprosy,
And subtle serpents gliding in her hair.
By day she woos me to the outer air,
    Ripe fruits, sweet flowers, and full satiety:
    But thro; the night a beast she grins at me,
A very monster void of love and prayer
By day she stands a lie: by night she stands
    In all the naked horror of the truth,
With pushing horns and clawed and
        clutching hands.
Is this a friend indeed, that I should sell
    My soul to her, give her my life and
        youth,
Till my feet, cloven too, take hold on hell?

Amor Mundi

'Oh where are you going with your love-
        locks flowing,
    On the west wind blowing along this
        valley track?'
'The downhill path is easy, come with me an
        it please ye,
    We shall escape the uphill by never
        turning back.'

So they two went together in glowing
        August weather,
    The honey-breathing heather lay to
        their left and right;
And dear she was to doat on, her swift feet
        seemed to float on
    The air like soft twin pigeons too
        sportive to alight.

'Oh what is that in heaven where grey
    cloud-flakes are seven,
    Where blackest clouds hang riven just
    at the rainy skirt?'
'Oh that's a meteor sent us, a message
    dumb, portentous,
    An undeciphered solemn signal of help
    or hurt.'

'Oh what is that glides quickly where velvet
    flowers grow thickly,
    Their scent comes rich and sickly?'
    'A scaled and hooded worm.'
'Oh what's that in the hollow, so pale I
    quake to follow?'
    'Oh that's a thin dead body which waits
    the eternal term.'

'Turn again, O my sweetest, – turn again,
    false and fleetest:
  This beaten way thou beatest, I fear, is
    hell's own track.'
'Nay, too steep for hill mounting; nay, too
    late for cost counting:
  This downhill path is easy, but there's
    no turning back.'

Proserpine, Dante Gabriel Rossetti

❧ DEATH ☙

Summer Is Ended

To think that this meaningless thing was
            ever a rose,
        Scentless, colourless, *this*!
    Will it ever be thus (who knows?)
        Thus with our bliss,
        If we wait till the close?

Though we care not to wait for the end,
            there comes the end,
        Sooner, later, at last,
    Which nothing can mar, nothing mend:
        An end locked fast,
        Bent we cannot re-bend.

A Dirge

Why were you born when the snow was
        falling?
You should have come to the cuckoo's
        calling,
Or when grapes are green in the cluster,
Or at least when lithe swallows muster
    For their far off flying
    From summer dying.

Why did you die when the lambs were
        cropping?
You should have died at the apples'
        dropping,
When the grasshopper comes to trouble,
And the wheat-fields are sodden stubble,
    And all winds go sighing
    For sweet things dying.

Backwards up the mossy glen
Turned and trooped the goblin men

Untitled

They lie at rest, our blessed dead;
The dews drop cool above their head,
They knew not when fleet summer fled.

Together all, yet each alone;
Each laid at rest beneath his own
Smooth turf or white allotted stone.

When shall our slumber sink so deep,
And eyes that wept and eyes that weep
Weep not in the sufficient sleep?

God be with you, our great and small,
Our loves, our best beloved of all,
Our own beyond the salt sea-wall.

Two Thoughts Of Death

I

Her heart that loved me once is rottenness
   Now and corruption; and her life is dead
   That was to have been one with mine, she
      said.
The earth must lie with such a cruel stress
On eyes whereon the white lid used to press;

Foul worms fill up her mouth so sweet and
        red;
Foul worms are underneath her graceful
        head;
Yet these, being born of her from
        nothingness,
These worms are certainly flesh of her flesh.
  How is it that the grass is rank and green
And the dew-dropping rose is brave and
        fresh
Above what was so sweeter far than they?

Life And Death

Life is not sweet. One day it will be sweet
    To shut our eyes and die:
Nor feel the wild flowers blow, nor birds
        dart by
    With flitting butterfly,
Nor grass grow long above our heads and
    feet,

Nor hear the happy lark that soars sky-high,
Nor sigh that spring is fleet and summer fleet,
    Nor mark the waxing wheat,
Nor know who sits in our accustomed seat.

Ripe fruits, sweet flowers, and full satiety

Life is not good. One day it will be good
    To die, then live again;
To sleep meanwhile; so, not to feel the wane
    Of shrunk leaves dropping in the
        wood,
Nor hear the foamy lashing of the main,
Nor mark the blackened bean-fields, nor,
        where stood
    Rich ranks of golden grain,
Only dead refuse stubble clothe the plain:
    Asleep from risk, asleep from pain.

After Death

The curtains were half drawn, the floor was
    swept
  And strewn with rushes, rosemary and
    may
  Lay thick upon the bed on which I lay,

Where through the lattice ivy-shadows
    crept.
He leaned above me, thinking that I slept
  And could not hear him; but I heard
    him say,
  'Poor child, poor child': and as he
    turned away

And all winds go sighing
For sweet things dying

Came a deep silence, and I knew he wept.
He did not touch the shroud, or raise the
    fold
  That hid my face, or take my hand in his,
    Or ruffle the smooth pillows for my
        head:
    He did not love me living; but once
        dead
He pitied me; and very sweet it is
To know he still is warm though I am cold.

A Portrait

She gave up beauty in her tender youth,
   Gave all her hope and joy and pleasant
           ways;
   She covered up her eyes lest they should
           gaze
On vanity, and chose the bitter truth.
Harsh towards herself, towards others full of
           ruth,
   Servant of servants, little known to praise,
   Long prayers and fasts trenched on her
           nights and days:
She schooled herself to sights and sounds
           uncouth
That with the poor and stricken she might
           make
   A home, until the least of all sufficed

Her wants; her own self learned she to
        forsake,
Counting all earthly gain but hurt and loss.
So with calm will she chose and bore the
        cross
  And hated all for love of Jesus Christ.
  21 *November* 1850.

II

They knelt in silent anguish by her bed,
  And could not weep; but calmly there she
        lay.
  All pain had left her; and the sun's last ray
Shone through upon her, warming into red
The shady curtains. In her heart she said:
  'Heaven opens; I leave these and go away;

The Bridegroom calls, – shall the Bride seek
        to stay?'
Then low upon her breast she bowed her
        head.
O lily flower, O gem of priceless worth,
  O dove with patient voice and patient
       eyes,
O fruitful vine amid a land of dearth,
  O maid replete with loving purities,
Thou bowedst down thy head with friends
       on earth
  To raise it with the saints in Paradise.

The Huguenot, John Everett Millais

Song

Two doves upon the selfsame branch,
   Two lilies on a single stem,
Two butterflies upon one flower: –
   Oh happy they who look on them!

Who look upon them hand in hand
   Flushed in the rosy summer light;
Who look upon them hand in hand,
   And never give a thought to night.

A Birthday

My heart is like a singing bird
    Whose nest is in a watered shoot:
My heart is like an apple-tree
    Whose boughs are bent with thickset
        fruit;
My heart is like a rainbow shell
    That paddles in a halcyon sea;
My heart is gladder than all these
    Because my love is come to me.

Raise me a dais of silk and down;
    Hang it with vair and purple dyes;
Carve it in doves and pomegranates,
    And peacocks with a hundred eyes;
Work it in gold and silver grapes,
    In leaves and silver fleurs-de-lys;
Because the birthday of my life
    Is come, my love is come to me.

My thirsty soul kept watch for one away

Grown And Flown

I loved my love from green of Spring
    Until sere Autumn's fall:
But now that leaves are withering
    How should one love at all?
    One heart's too small
For hunger, cold, love, everything.

I loved my love on sunny days
    Until late Summer's wane;
But now that frost begins to glaze
    How should one love again?
    Nay, love and pain
Walk wide apart in diverse ways.

I loved my love alas to see
    That this should be, alas!
I thought that this could scarcely be,
    Yet has it come to pass:
    Sweet sweet love was,
Now bitter bitter grown to me.

Maude Clare

Out of the church she followed them
    With a lofty step mien:
His bride was like a village maid,
    Maud Clare was like a queen.

'Son Thomas,' his lady mother said,
    With smiles, almost with tears:
'May Nell and you but live as true
    As we have done for years;

'Your father thirty years ago
    Had just your tale to tell;
But he was not so pale as you,
    Nor I so pale as Nell.'

My lord was pale with inward strife,
    And Nell was pale with pride;
My lord gazed long on pale Maude Clare
    Or ever he kissed the bride.

'Lo, I have brought my gift, my lord,
    Have brought my gift,' she said:
'To bless the hearth, to bless the board,
    To bless the marriage-bed.

'Here's my half of the golden chain
    You wore about your neck,
That day we waded ankle-deep
    For lilies in the beck.

'Here's my half of the faded leaves
    We plucked from budding bough,
With feet amongst the lily leaves, –
    The lilies are budding now.'

He strove to match her scorn with scorn,
    He faltered in his place:
'Lady,' he said, – 'Maude Clare,' he said, –
    'Maude Clare': – and hid his face.

She turned to Nell: 'My Lady Nell,
    I have a gift for you;
Though, were it fruit, the bloom were
        gone,
    Or, were it flowers, the dew.

'Take my share of a fickle heart,
    Mine of a paltry love:
Take it or leave it as you will,
    I wash my hands thereof.'

'And what you leave,' said Nell, 'I'll take,
    And what you spurn I'll wear;
For he's my lord for better and worse,
    And him I love, Maude Clare.

'Yea though you're taller by the head,
    More wise, and much more fair,
I'll love him till he loves me best –
    Me best of all, Maude Clare.'

. . . and I felt my hair
Put on a glory, and my soul expand

Twice

I took my heart in my hand,
   (O my love, O my love),
I said: Let me fall or stand,
   Let me live or die,
But this once hear me speak
   (O my love, O my love) –
Yet a woman's words are weak;
   You should speak, not I.

You took my heart in your hand
   With a friendly smile,
With a critical eye you scanned,
   Then set it down,
And said: It is still unripe,
   Better wait awhile;
Wait while the skylarks pipe,
   Till the corn grows brown.

As you set it down it broke –
    Broke, but I did not wince;
I smiled at the speech you spoke,
    At your judgment that I heard:
But I have not often smiled
    Since then, nor questioned since,
Nor cared for corn-flowers wild,
    Nor sung with the singing bird.

I take my heart in my hand,
    O my God, O my God,
My broken heart in my hand:
    Thou hast seen, judge Thou.
My hope was written on sand,
    O my God, O my God:
Now let Thy judgment stand
    Yea, judge me now.

Falling Leaves, John Melhuish Strudwick

This contemned of a man,
    This marred one heedless day,
This heard take Thou to scan
    Both within and without:
Refine with fire its gold,
    Purge Thou its dross away –
Yea hold it in Thy hold,
    Whence none can pluck it out.

I take my heart in my hand –
    I shall not die, but live –
Before Thy face I stand;
    I, for Thou callest such:
All that I have I bring,
    All that I am I give,
Smile Thou and I shall sing,
    But shall not question much.

'No, Thank You, John'

I never said I loved you, John;
    Why will you tease me day by day,
And wax a weariness to think upon
    With always 'do' and 'pray'?

You know I never loved you, John;
    No fault of mine made me your toast:
Why will you haunt me with a face as wan
    As shows an hour-old ghost?

I dare say Meg or Moll would take
    Pity upon you, if you'd ask:
And pray don't remain single for my sake
    Who can't perform that task.

I have no heart? – Perhaps I have not;
    But then you're mad to take offence
That I don't give you what I have not got:
    Use your own common sense.

Let bygones be bygones:
    Don't call me false, who owed not to be
        true:
I'd rather answer 'No' to fifty Johns
    Than answer 'Yes' to you.

A Triad

Three sang of love together: one with lips
    Crimson, with cheeks and bosom in a
        glow,
Flushed to the yellow hair and finger-tips;
    And one there sang who soft and smooth
        as snow
    Bloomed like a tinted hyacinth at a show;
And one was blue with famine after love,
    Who like a harpstring snapped rang harsh
        and low
The burden of what those were singing of.
One shamed herself in love; one temperately

Summer is gone with all its roses,
Its sun and perfumes and sweet flowers

Grew gross in soulless love, a sluggish
        wife;
One famished died for love. Thus two of
        three
    Took death for love and won him after
        strife;
One droned in sweetness like a fattened bee:
    All on the threshold, yet all short of life.
    18 *December* 1856.

A Pause

They made the chamber sweet with flowers
        and leaves,
    And the bed sweet with flowers on which
        I lay;
    While my soul, love-bound, loitered on
        its way.
I did not hear the birds about the eaves,
Nor hear the reapers talk among the sheaves:
    Only my soul kept watch from day to day,
    My thirsty soul kept watch for one away: —

The March of the Seasons, Charles Edward Hallé

Perhaps he loves, I thought, remembers,
        grieves.
At length there came the step upon the stair,
  Upon the lock the old familiar hand:
Then first my spirit seemed to scent the air
  Of Paradise; then first the tardy sand
Of time ran golden; and I felt my hair
  Put on a glory, and my soul expand.

A Better Resurrection

I have no wit, no words, no tears;
    My heart within me like a stone
Is numbed too much for hopes or fears.
    Look right, look left, I dwell alone;
I lift mine eyes, but dimmed with grief
    No everlasting hills I see;
My life is in the falling leaf:
        O Jesus, quicken me.

My life is like a faded leaf,
    My harvest dwindled to a husk:
Truly my life is void and brief
    And tedious in the barren dusk;

My life is like a frozen thing,
   No bud nor greenness can I see;
Yet rise it shall – the sap of Spring;
   O Jesus, rise in me.

My life is like a broken bowl,
   A broken bowl that cannot hold
One drop of water for my soul
   Or cordial in the searching cold;

Cast in the fire the perished thing;
   Melt and remould it, till it be
A royal cup for Him, my King:
   O Jesus, drink of me.

Beauty Is Vain

While roses are so red,
  While lilies are so white,
Shall a woman exalt her face
  Because it gives delight?
She's not so sweet as a rose,
  A lily's straighter than she,
And if she were as red or white
  She'd be but one of three.

Whether she flush in love's summer
  Or in its winter grow pale,
Whether she flaunt her beauty
  Or hide it away in a veil,
Be she red or white
  And stand she erect or bowed,
Time will win the race he runs with her,
  And hide her away in a shroud.

Truly my life is void and brief
And tedious in the barren dusk

The Bourne

Underneath the growing grass,
   Underneath the living flowers,
   Deeper than the sound of showers:
   There we shall not count the hours
By the shadows as they pass.

Youth and health will be but vain,
   Beauty reckoned of no worth:
   There a very little girth
   Can hold round what once the earth
Seemed too narrow to contain.

One Certainty

Vanity of vanities, the Preacher saith,
    All things are vanity. The eye and ear
    Cannot be filled with what they see and
        hear.
Like early dew, or like the sudden breath
Of wind, or like the grass that withereth,
    Is man, tossed to and fro by hope and fear:

The Soul of the Rose,
John William Waterhouse

So little joy hath he, so little cheer,
Till all things end in the long dust of death.
To-day is still the same as yesterday,
  To-morrow also even as one of them;
    And there is nothing new under the
      sun:
    Until the ancient race of Time be run,
The old thorns shall grow out of the old
      stem,
And morning shall be cold and twilight grey.

Withering

Fade, tender lily,
    Fade, O crimson rose,
Fade every flower,
    Sweetest flower that blows.

Go, chilly autumn,
    Come, O winter cold;
Let the green stalks die away
    Into common mould.

Birth follows hard on death,
    Life on withering:
Hasten, we will come the sooner
    Back to pleasant spring.

Bitter For Sweet

Summer is gone with all its roses,
    Its sun and perfumes and sweet flowers,
    Its warm air and refreshing showers:
      And even Autumn closes.
Yea, Autumn's chilly self is going,
    And Winter comes which is yet colder;
    Each day the hoar-frost waxes bolder,
      And the last buds cease blowing.

Endurance

Yes, I too could face death and never shrink.
  But it is harder to bear hated life;
    To strive with hands and knees weary of
        strife;
To drag the heavy chain whose every link
Galls to the bone; to stand upon the brink
    Of the deep grave, nor drowse tho' it be
        rife

My heart is breaking for a little love

With sleep; to hold with steady hand the
        knife
Nor strike home: – this is courage, as I think.
Surely to suffer is more than to do.
    To do is quickly done: to suffer is
        Longer and fuller of heart-sicknesses.
    Each day's experience testifies of this.
Good deeds are many, but good lives are
        few:
    Thousands taste the full cup;
      who drains the lees?

Vanity Of Vanities

Ah woe is me for pleasure that is vain,
    Ah woe is me for glory that is past!
    Pleasure that bringeth sorrow at the last,
Glory that at the last bringeth no gain.
So saith the sinking heart; and so again
    It shall say till the mighty angel-blast
    Is blown, making the sun and moon
        aghast,

And showering down the stars like sudden
  rain.
And evermore men shall go fearfully,
  Bending beneath their weight of
    heaviness;
And ancient men shall lie down wearily,
  And strong men shall rise up in
    weariness:
Yea even the young shall answer sighingly,
  Saying one to another 'How vain it is!'

May

I cannot tell you how it was;
But this I know: it came to pass —
Upon a bright and breezy day
When May was young, ah pleasant May!
As yet the poppies were not born
Between the blades of tender corn;
The last eggs had not hatched as yet,
Nor any bird forgone its mate.

I cannot tell you what it was;
But this I know: it did but pass.
It passed away with sunny May,
With all sweet things it passed away,
And left me old, and cold, and grey.

Song

Oh roses for the flush of youth,
  And laurel for the perfect prime;
But pluck an ivy branch for me
  Grown old before my time.

Oh violets for the grave of youth,
  And bay for those dead in their prime;
Give me the withered leaves I chose
  Before in the old time.

Somewhere Or Other

Somewhere or other there must surely be
The face not seen, the voice not heard,
The heart that not yet – never yet ah me!
Made answer to my word.

Somewhere or other, may be near or far;
Past land and sea, clean out of sight;
Beyond the wandering moon, beyond the
star
That tracks her night by night.

Somewhere or other, may be far or near;
With just a wall, a hedge, between;
With just the last leaves of the dying year
Fallen on a turf grown green.

What Would I Give!

What would I give for a heart of flesh to
      warm me through,
Instead of this heart of stone ice-cold
      whatever I do!
Hard and cold and small, of all hearts the
      worst of all.

What would I give for words, if only words
      would come!
But now in its misery my spirit has fallen
      dumb.
O merry friends, go your way, I have never a
      word to say.

What would I give for tears! not smiles but
      scalding tears,
To wash the black mark clean, and to thaw
      the frost of years,
To wash the stain ingrain, and to make me
      clean again.

In An Artist's Studio

One face looks out from all his canvases,
  One selfsame figure sits or walks or leans:
  We found her hidden just behind those
      screens,
That mirror gave back all her loveliness.
A queen in opal or in ruby dress,
  A nameless girl in freshest summer-greens,
  A saint, an angel – every canvas means
The same one meaning, neither more nor
      less.
He feeds upon her face by day and night,

And she with true kind eyes looks back on
        him,
Fair as the moon and joyful as the light:
  Not wan with waiting, not with sorrow
        dim;
Not as she is, but was when hope shone
        bright;
  Not as she is, but as she fills his dream.

From The Antique

It's a weary life, it is, she said:
  Doubly blank in a woman's lot:
I wish and I wish I were a man:
  Or, better than any being, were not:

Were nothing at all in all the world.
  Not a body and not a soul:
Not so much as a grain of dust
  Or drop of water from pole to pole.

Still the world would wag on the same,
　　Still the seasons go and come:
Blossoms bloom as in days of old,
　　Cherries ripen and wild bees hum.

None would miss me in all the world,
　　How much less would care or weep:
I should be nothing, while all the rest
　　Would wake and weary and fall asleep.

Promises Like Pie-Crust

Promise me no promises,
  So will I not promise you:
Keep we both our liberties,
  Never false and never true:
Let us hold the die uncast,
  Free to come as free to go:

For I cannot know your past,
  And of mine what can you know?

You, so warm, may once have been
  Warmer towards another one:
I, so cold, may once have seen
  Sunlight, once have felt the sun:

Who shall show us if it was
   Thus indeed in time of old?
Fades the image from the glass,
   And the fortune is not told.

If you promised, you might grieve
   For lost liberty again:
If I promised, I believe
   I should fret to break the chain.
Let us be the friends we were,
   Nothing more but nothing less:
Many thrive on frugal fare
   Who would perish of excess.

L. E. L.

'Whose heart was breaking for a little love.'
Downstairs I laugh, I sport and jest with all;
   But in my solitary room above
I turn my face in silence to the wall;
   My heart is breaking for a little love.
      Though winter frosts are done,
      And birds pair every one,
And leaves peep out, for springtide is begun.

I feel no spring, while spring is well-high
        blown,
   I find no nest, while nests are in the grove:
Woe's me for mine own heart that dwells
        alone,
   My heart that breaketh for a little love.
      While golden in the sun
      Rivulets rise and run,
While lilies bud, for springtide is begun.

A Wish

I wish I were a little bird
    That out of sight doth soar;
I wish I were a song once heard
    But often pondered o'er,
Or shadow of a lily stirred
    By wind upon the floor,
Or echo of a loving word
    Worth all that went before,
Or memory of a hope deferred
    That springs again no more.

Fata Morgana

A blue-eyed phantom far before
    Is laughing, leaping toward the sun:
Like lead I chase it evermore,
    I pant and run.

It breaks the sunlight bound on bound:
    Goes singing as it leaps along
To sheep-bells with a dreamy sound
    A dreamy song.

I laugh, it is so brisk and gay;
    It is so far before, I weep:
I hope I shall lie down some day,
    Lie down and sleep.

Couplet

'Come cheer up, my lads, 'tis to glory we
steer' –
As the soldier remarked whose post lay in
the rear.